SPOTLIGHT ON SPACE SCIENCE

JOURNEY TO URANUS

VALERIE HUNTER

New York

Published in 2015 by The Rosen Publishing Group, Inc.
29 East 21st Street, New York, NY 10010

First Edition

Editor: Susan Meyer
Book Design: Kris Everson

Photo Credits: Cover (main), p. 11 Stocktrek Images; cover (small planet image), pp. 5, 15, 23, 29 NASA; p. 7 ESO/L. Calçada - ESO; p. 9 Baris Simsek; p. 13 Lawrence Sromovsky, University of Wisconsin-Madison/W.M. Keck Observatory; p. 17 Science Source; p. 19 Bibi Saint-Pol; p. 21 NASA/JPL; p. 25 W. M. Keck Observatory (Marcos van Dam); p. 27 CARLOS CLARIVAN/ SCIENCE PHOTO LIBRARY.

Library of Congress Cataloging-in-Publication Data

Hunter, Valerie.
Journey to Uranus / by Valerie Hunter.
p. cm. — (Spotlight on space science)
Includes index.
ISBN 978-1-4994-0379-4 (pbk.)
ISBN 978-1-4994-0408-1 (6-pack)
ISBN 978-1-4994-0434-0 (library binding)
1. Voyager Project — Juvenile literature. 2. Uranus (Planet) — Juvenile literature. I. Title.
QB681.H868 2015
523.47—d23

Manufactured in the United States of America

CPSIA Compliance Information: Batch #CW15PK: For Further Information contact Rosen Publishing, New York, New York at 1-800-237-9932

CONTENTS

FAR, FAR AWAY

CHAPTER 1

Uranus is the seventh **planet** from the Sun in our **solar system**. It is a huge, cold world that **orbits** the Sun at an average distance of 1.7 billion miles (2.7 billion km).

Mercury, Venus, Mars, Jupiter, and Saturn, which are the five planets nearest to Earth, can be observed with the naked eye. The earliest humans would have seen these planets in the night sky. **Astronomers** did not know Uranus existed, however, until telescopes became available.

Today, we know that huge, distant Uranus is blue because of the amount of methane gas in its **atmosphere**. We also know it has many moons and a system of dark, icy rings encircling it. There are many mysteries still to be unraveled, however, because unlike the planets closer to Earth, Uranus

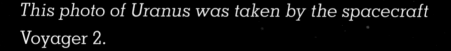

This photo of Uranus was taken by the spacecraft Voyager 2.

is difficult to see, even with the most powerful telescopes. Also, unlike planets such as Venus or Mars that have been visited by spacecraft and robots, only one spacecraft, NASA'S *Voyager 2,* has ever visited this faraway planet.

HOW THE PLANETS WERE FORMED

CHAPTER 2

About 5 billion years ago, the Sun, Earth, Uranus, and everything else in the solar system did not exist.

The chemical ingredients to make the Sun, eight planets and their moons, **dwarf planets**, **asteroids**, and every other object in the solar system did exist, however. These ingredients were floating in space in a vast cloud of gas and dust.

Over millions of years, part of the cloud began to collapse on itself, forming a massive rotating sphere, or ball. Around the sphere, a spinning disk formed from the remaining gas and dust. The material in the sphere was pressed together by **gravity**, causing it to heat up and pressure to build. Eventually, the heat and pressure became so great that the sphere ignited. In that moment, a new star, our Sun, was born!

Gas and dust continued to spin in a disk around the Sun. Over time, material in the disk clumped together to form all the objects in the solar system. One of the objects that formed on the outer edges of the spinning disk was the planet Uranus.

A solar system forms when the gases and matter around a star flatten out into a huge disk.

CHAPTER 3

The solar system is measured in billions of miles (km). It can be hard to imagine distances that are so vast. There is a fun way, however, to experience the scale of the solar system and visualize the size of the planets in comparison with each other.

If you take a bowling ball and imagine that it is the Sun, then small planets such as Mercury and Mars and the dwarf planet Pluto could be represented by pinheads. Venus and Earth would be the size of a peppercorn. Uranus and Neptune would be the size of a pea. Saturn would be the size of a marble, and giant Jupiter would be the size of a chestnut.

In this scaled-down version of the solar system, tiny pinhead Mercury, the closest planet to the Sun, is 10 yards (9 m) from the bowling-ball Sun. Earth would be 26 yards (24 m) from the

Uranus is the seventh-farthest planet from the Sun in our solar system.

bowling-ball Sun. Distant pea Uranus would be 496 yards (454 m) from the bowling-ball Sun. Most amazingly, pinhead Pluto would be about the length of 10 football fields away from the bowling-ball Sun!

URANUS'S ORBIT AND ROTATION
CHAPTER 4

Like our Earth and the other planets and objects in the solar system, Uranus orbits the Sun. As it travels through space, it is moving at about 15,200 miles per hour (24,462 km/h).

The time period that it takes a planet to make one full orbit of the Sun is called a year. Earth orbits the Sun once every 365 days, so a year on Earth lasts for 365 days. Uranus is much farther from the Sun than Earth, however, so its journey takes longer. In fact, it takes Uranus 30,687 days to make one full orbit. So a year on Uranus actually lasts for 84 Earth years! During that long year, Uranus makes a journey of 11,201,335,967 miles (18,026,802,831 km).

As the planets in the solar system orbit the Sun, each one also rotates, or spins, on its

Uranus is orbited by several moons. This view of the planet is seen from the grooved surface of its moon Miranda.

As a planet rotates on its axis, it could be described as spinning like a top.

The planets are slightly tilted, so each planet's axis is also at a slightly tilted angle. For example, Earth's axis is tilted at 23.5 degrees. Even with a slight tilt, most of the planets still rotate in a nearly upright way. Uranus, however, is so tilted on its axis that it is actually spinning on its side!

No one knows how Uranus came to be spinning so differently from all the other planets. The most popular theory, though, is that at some time, billions of years ago, Uranus was hit by another enormous space object. Before the collision, Uranus was spinning in an upright position, like Earth. The impact of the collision was so great, though, that it knocked Uranus onto its side, leaving it to become the sideways-spinning planet.

*This photo from the Keck **Observatory** shows how Uranus rotates on its side.*

A LONG WINTER

CHAPTER 6

Just like the other planets in the solar system, Uranus has seasons, days, and nights. Each season on Uranus lasts for about 21 years, however, because it takes the planet 84 years to make one orbit of the Sun.

During one of Uranus's 21-year-long seasons, the equator faces the Sun, and the entire planet experiences autumn. As the planet moves through its orbit into winter, the north pole points away from the Sun, and the planet's northern **hemisphere** has about 21 years of winter. As the north experiences winter, the southern hemisphere has a long summer. During the next 21 years, the entire planet passes through its spring, and then the northern hemisphere experiences a 21-year summer, while the south has a long winter.

Uranus orbits the Sun from an average distance of 1,787,000,000 miles (2,877,000,000 km).

URANUS'S LAYERS

CHAPTER 7

As one of the gas giant planets, Uranus does not have a solid surface. It is a massive ball made mostly of gases and liquids.

Surrounding Uranus is an atmosphere that is made up mostly of hydrogen and helium. The atmosphere also contains small amounts of methane, water, and the gas ammonia. It is the methane in Uranus's atmosphere that gives the planet its blue color. As light from the Sun penetrates the planet's atmosphere, clouds beneath the atmosphere reflect the light back out. Light is made up of different colors, though, and the methane gas in the atmosphere absorbs the red parts of the light. It then allows only the blues and greens to be reflected, so we see Uranus as a blue-colored planet.

Beneath Uranus's atmosphere is a deep layer of icy liquids including water, liquid methane, and

Taken by a Japenese telescope, this image captures methane in the atmosphere of Uranus in blue.

ammonia. Deep inside the planet, scientists believe there is a solid core of rock.

AN EXCITING DISCOVERY

Uranus was the first new planet to be discovered after the invention of the telescope in the early 1600s.

William Herschel was a German-born British astronomer who built his own telescopes. In March 1781, Herschel was studying space, looking for stars. When he first observed Uranus, he believed it was a star or perhaps a comet.

Herschel was not the first astronomer to have seen Uranus. Others had viewed it through telescopes in the previous 100 years and had also believed it was a star. After further studies, Herschel was able to confirm that the object he'd first seen on March 13, 1781, was in fact a planet orbiting the Sun beyond the orbit of Saturn.

Herschel wanted to name his planet Georgian Sidus, which is Latin for the "Georgian Star," in honor of the British king at the time, George III.

Uranus was the Greek god of the skies and heavens. He was married to the goddess Gaia, or Earth.

It was eventually named Uranus, however, after the Greek god of the sky.

MANY MOONS

A moon is a naturally occurring satellite that orbits a planet. Mercury has no moons, Earth has one, and Mars has two. Uranus has 27 known moons. There could still be more to be discovered, however!

Uranus's five largest moons were the first to be observed by astronomers using telescopes from Earth. In 1787, William Herschel discovered the planet's two largest moons, Titania and Oberon. Even though Titania is the planet's largest moon, it is still only half the size of our moon, with a diameter of just 980 miles (1,578 km).

In 1851, British astronomer William Lassell discovered the moons Ariel and Umbriel. Nearly 100 years then passed before American astronomer Gerard Kuiper discovered Miranda in 1948. For several decades, Uranus had only five known moons, and it would be 1986, when

Uranus's five largest moons from clockwise starting at the top center (not to scale): Oberon, Titania, Miranda, Ariel, and Umbriel.

Voyager 2 visited the planet, before more moons were discovered.

CHAPTER 10

When NASA's *Voyager 2* spacecraft flew by Uranus in 1986, it discovered 10 more moons.

Since *Voyager 2's* discoveries, another 12 small moons have been discovered using the Hubble Space Telescope. Today, we know of 27 moons orbiting Uranus. Finding these smaller moons has been difficult. They are nearly 2 billion miles (3 billion km) from Earth and have diameters as small as 10 miles (16 km). Scientists believe they could be asteroids that have been pulled into orbit around Uranus by the planet's gravity.

In addition to discovering new moons, *Voyager 2* and the Hubble Space Telescope have allowed us to see and find out more about the planet's largest moons. We know they are made of ice and rock. We know Oberon has a mountain that

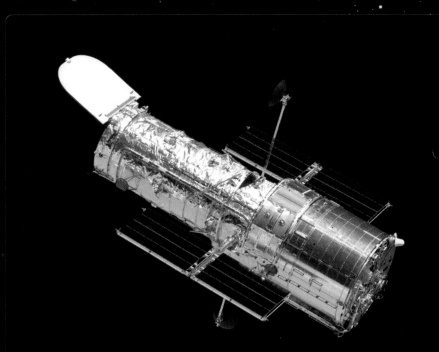

The Hubble Space Telescope was launched into orbit around Earth in 1990.

is 3.7 miles (6 km) high and that Miranda has giant canyons that are 12 times as deep as the Grand Canyon!

FINDING THE RINGS

Astronomers had been studying Uranus for nearly 200 years when they discovered the surprising secret that it has rings.

In 1977, two groups of astronomers were observing Uranus as it passed in front of a star. One team was at the Perth Observatory in Australia. The other team was aboard the Kuiper Airborne Observatory (KAO). The KAO was an aircraft fitted out to be a flying observatory that could fly 9 miles (14 km) above Earth's surface. At this height, there is less interference from clouds and Earth's atmosphere, so astronomers are able to view space more clearly.

As the two teams of astronomers watched Uranus pass in front of the star, the star's light was blocked in an unexpected way. The objects causing the blockage of light were rings encircling the planet. Today, thanks to *Voyager 2*'s visit to

This image shows Uranus and its rings in infrared. These wavelengths make it possible to see the planet's rings clearly.

Uranus in 1986 and observations by the Hubble Space Telescope, we know that Uranus has at least 13 rings encircling it.

EXPLORING THE OUTER SOLAR SYSTEM

CHAPTER 12

In 1977, NASA'S *Voyager 1* and *Voyager 2* spacecraft were launched on a mission to visit the solar system's outer planets.

The mission was possible because the orbits of the planets Jupiter, Saturn, Uranus, and Neptune were **aligned** in a way that only happens every 175 years. This rare alignment allowed the *Voyagers* to visit a planet and then use the gravity of that planet like a slingshot to propel them onto the next planet. Originally, the plan was that the two spacecraft would visit Jupiter and Saturn. The *Voyagers* functioned so successfully, however, that it became possible to extend their missions.

Voyager 2 launched from the Kennedy Space Center at Cape Canaveral, Florida, on August 20, 1977. *Voyager 1* actually launched after *Voyager 2* on September 5, 1977.

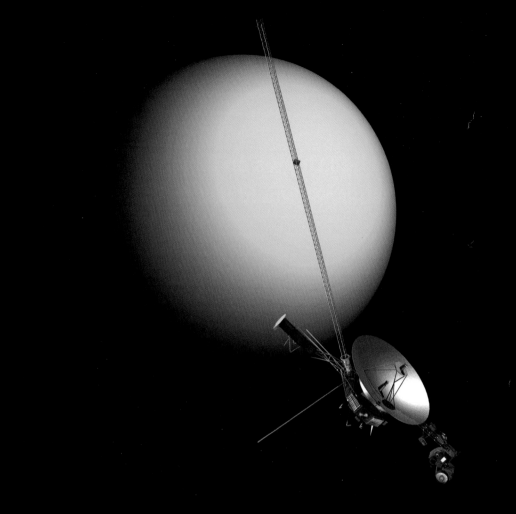

Much of what we now know about Uranus, its moons, and its rings come from Voyager 2's visit to the planet in 1986.

Voyager 2 **reached Jupiter in July 1979 and Saturn in August 1981. After four years in space, the spacecraft's instruments were still functioning well, so it was sent on its way to Uranus.**

CHAPTER 13

Voyager 2 reached Uranus on January 24, 1986. Its flyby of the planet would last for just five and a half hours.

At its closest, *Voyager 2* was 44,000 miles (71,000 km) from Uranus. During the spacecraft's incredibly short visit to the planet, *Voyager 2* took many photographs and discovered 10 new moons and two new rings. It sent data back to Earth about the gases that make up the planet's atmosphere, took temperature readings, and recorded wind speeds on the planet of 450 miles per hour (724 km/h). *Voyager 2* also discovered an ocean of boiling water about 500 miles (800 km) below the planet's cloud tops.

After visiting Uranus, *Voyager 2* continued on to Neptune. Today, *Voyager 1* and *Voyager 2* are still exploring the outer reaches of the solar system.

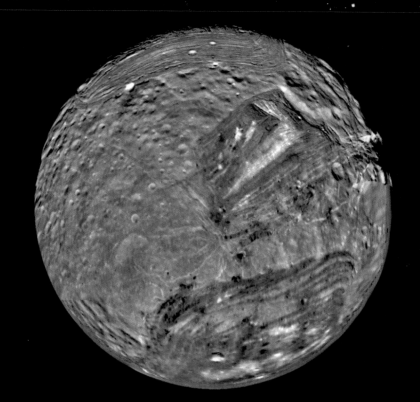

This photo of the moon Miranda was taken by Voyager 2 in 1986.

When will another spacecraft visit Uranus? There are several missions under discussion, but it will be at least another decade or two before we get to see Uranus up close again.

GLOSSARY

aligned: Arranged to form a line.

asteroid: A small, rocky body in space.

astronomer: A person who studies stars, planets, and other objects in outer space.

atmosphere: The gases that surround a planet or star.

axis: The imaginary straight line that something, such as the Earth, turns around.

dwarf planet: A body in space that orbits the Sun and is shaped like a sphere but is not large enough to disturb other objects from its orbit.

gravity: The natural force that causes planets and stars to move towards each other.

hemisphere: Half of a planet.

observatory: A building from which scientists study and watch the sky.

orbit: To move in a circle around something. Also, the path of an object that moves in a circle around another object.

planet: A large, round object in space that travels around a star.

solar system: The Sun, planets, moons, and other space objects.

FOR MORE INFORMATION

BOOKS

Lawrence, Ellen. *Uranus: The Sideways-Spinning Planet*.
New York, NY: Ruby Tuesday Books, Ltd., 2013.

Roza, Greg. *Uranus: The Ice Planet*. New York, NY: Gareth
Stevens Publishing, 2011.

Taylor-Butler, Christine. *Planet Uranus*. New York, NY:
Children's Press, 2014.

WEBSITES

Due to the changing nature of Internet links, PowerKids Press has developed
an online list of websites related to the subject of this book. This site is updated
regularly. Please use this link to access the list: www.powerkidslinks.com/soss/uran

INDEX